Skeletons

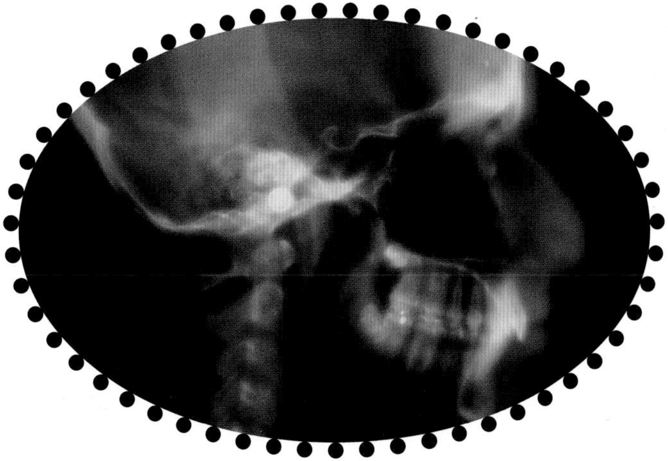

Diana Noonan

OXFORD
UNIVERSITY PRESS

Contents

Introduction	3
The Human Skeleton	4
Bones	5
Joints	9
Skull	12
Spine	13
Pelvis	14
Ribs	15
Arms and Hands	16
Legs and Feet	17
Broken Bones	18
Types of Fracture	19
Glossary	23
Index	24

Introduction

A skeleton is a firm, hard framework that supports the body of an animal or plant. Humans and most other animals have a bony skeleton inside the body, covered by skin. It grows as the body grows.

You cannot see your skeleton, but you can see and feel the shapes of some bones through your skin.

Your skeleton protects the parts of you which are inside, like your heart. Your skeleton also holds your body in shape, just like a tent pole holds a tent in place. Without a skeleton you would be as floppy as a jellyfish!

The Human Skeleton

- collar bone
- shoulder blade
- spine
- wrist
- hand
- fingers
- knee joint
- toes
- foot
- thigh bone
- hip joint
- pelvis
- ribs
- breast bone
- jaw bone
- skull

Bones

A human skeleton is made up of 206 bones of all shapes and sizes. Babies are born with up to 300 bones, but some of these join together as children grow up.

Interesting Bone Facts

The smallest bone in the body is the stirrup bone. This bone is found in the ear. It is half the size of a grain of rice.

Your skeleton does not stop growing until you are about 20 years old.

Like a giraffe, you have seven bones in your neck, though the giraffe's bones are a little larger.

Your nose has no bones in it.

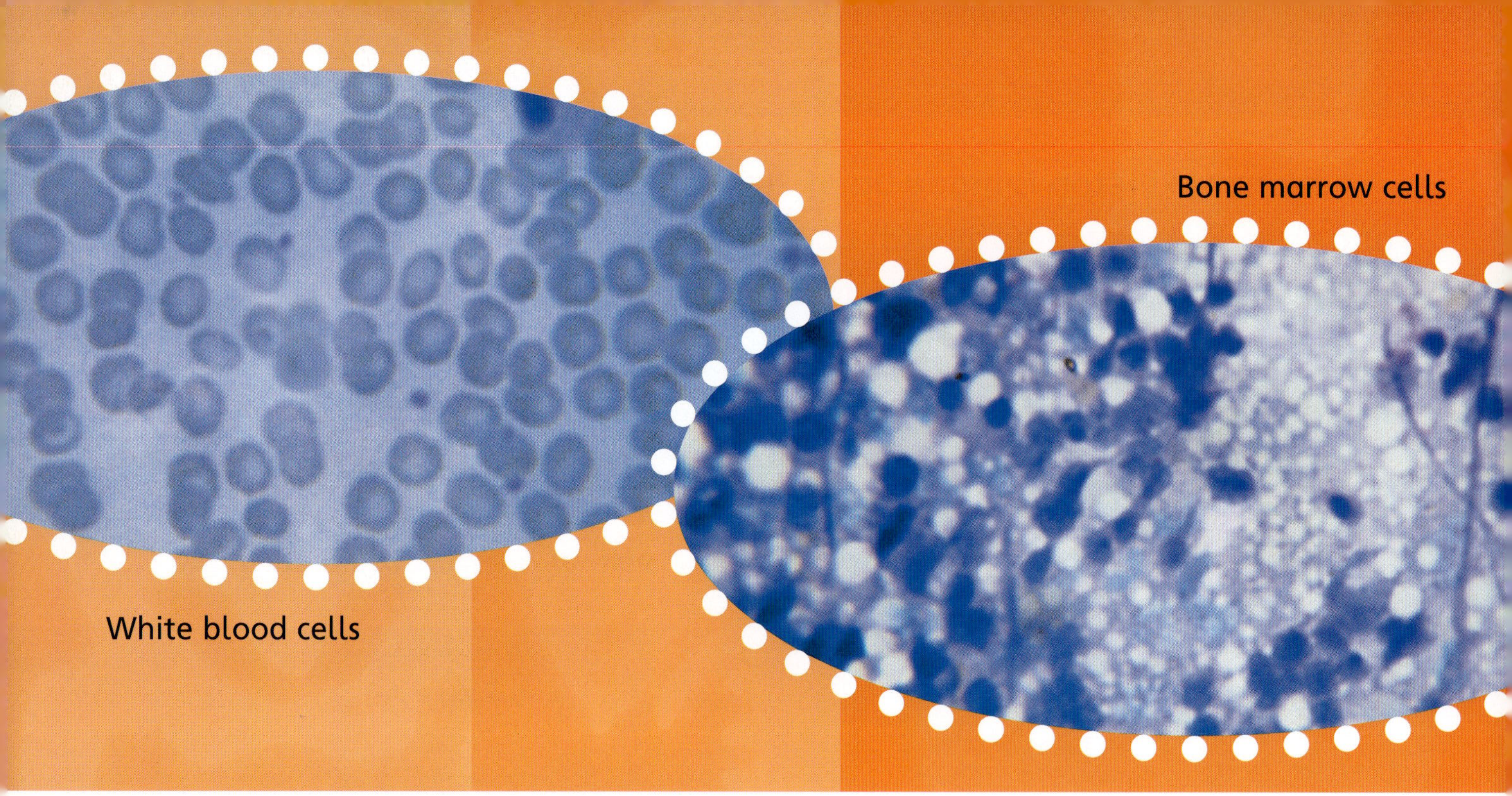

Living bones in the body are a creamy yellow colour. They are strong but they can bend very slightly. Living bones have blood vessels and **nerves** in them. Some have bone marrow inside them. The bone marrow makes special white blood **cells** that help protect the body from illness.

White blood cells

Bone marrow cells

Dead bones, such as animal bones you might find in a field or on a beach, are white and **brittle**.

The skeleton of an elephant

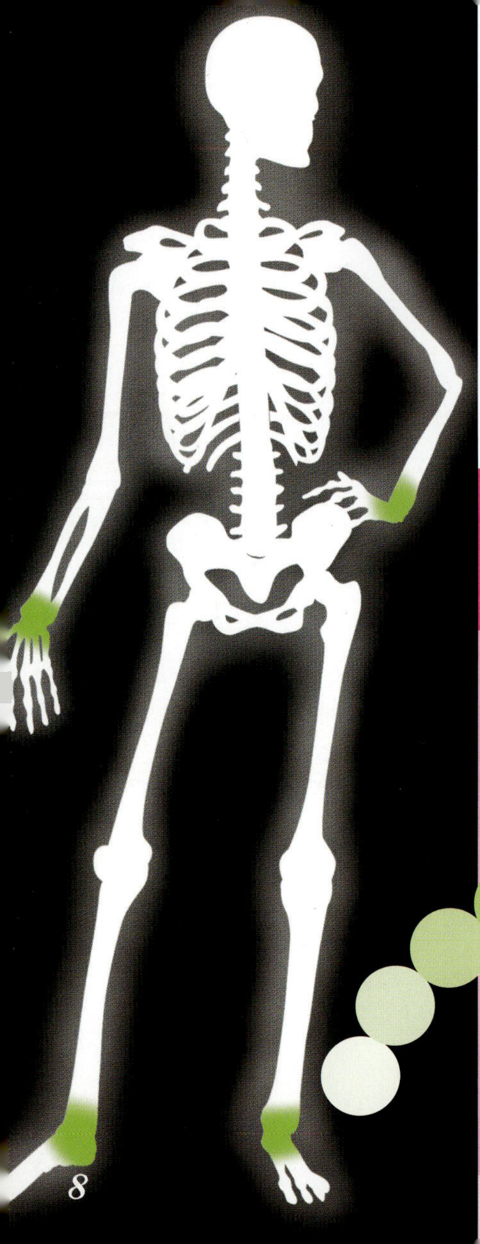

Adults' bones are soft and spongy on the inside but hard on the outside. Newborn babies have many bones that are soft and rubbery. These soft bones are called **cartilage**. Most cartilage slowly changes into hard bone as babies grow. Wrist and ankle bones are some of the last to harden.

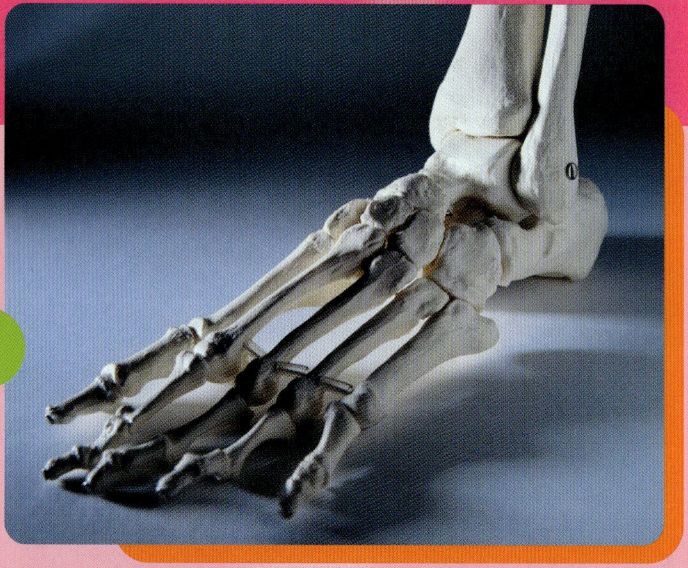

Foot and ankle bones

Joints

An X-ray of a knee joint

Knees bend in this direction.

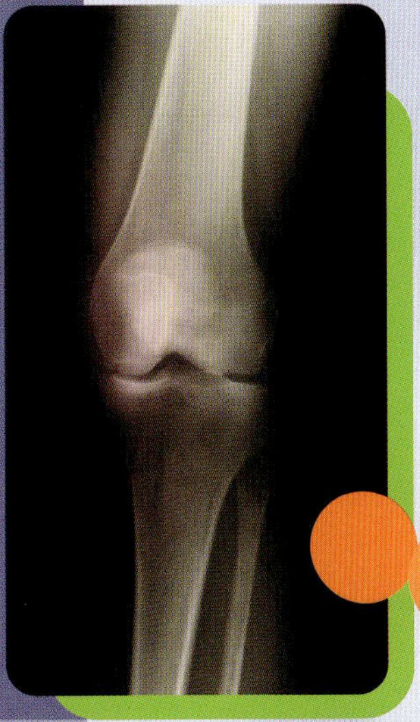

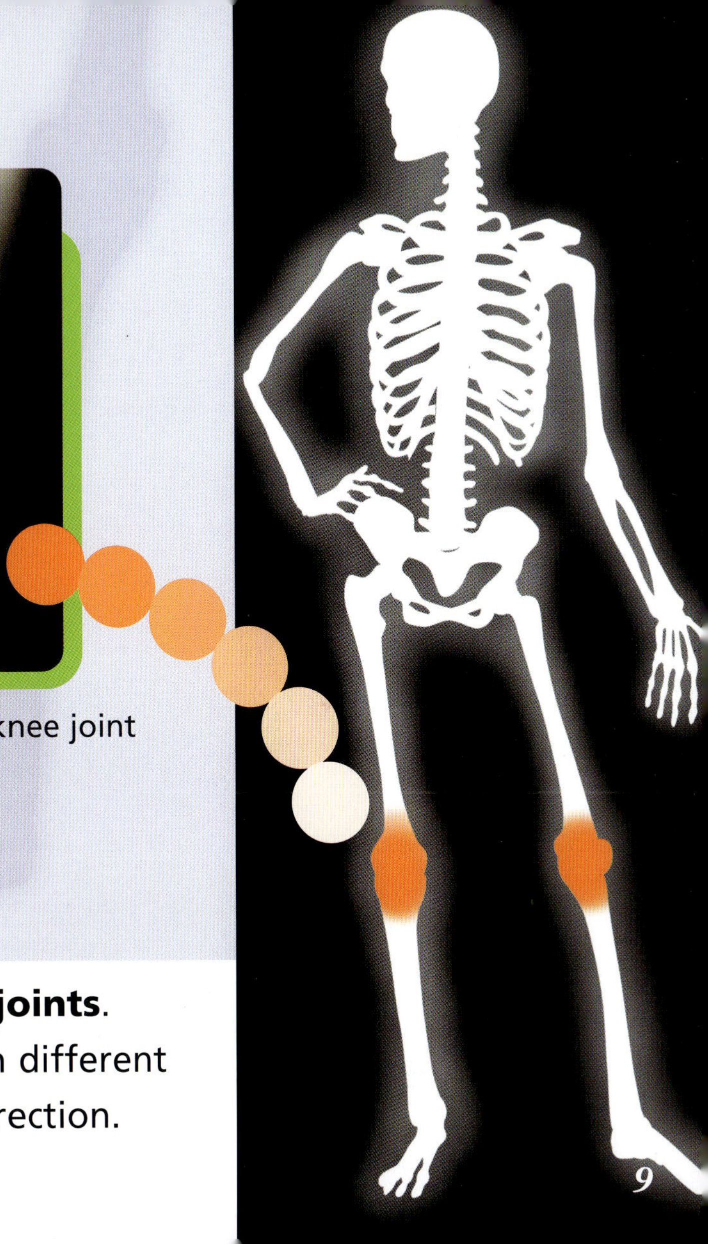

The places where bones meet are called **joints**. Different kinds of joints help bones move in different ways. Joints like knees only bend in one direction.

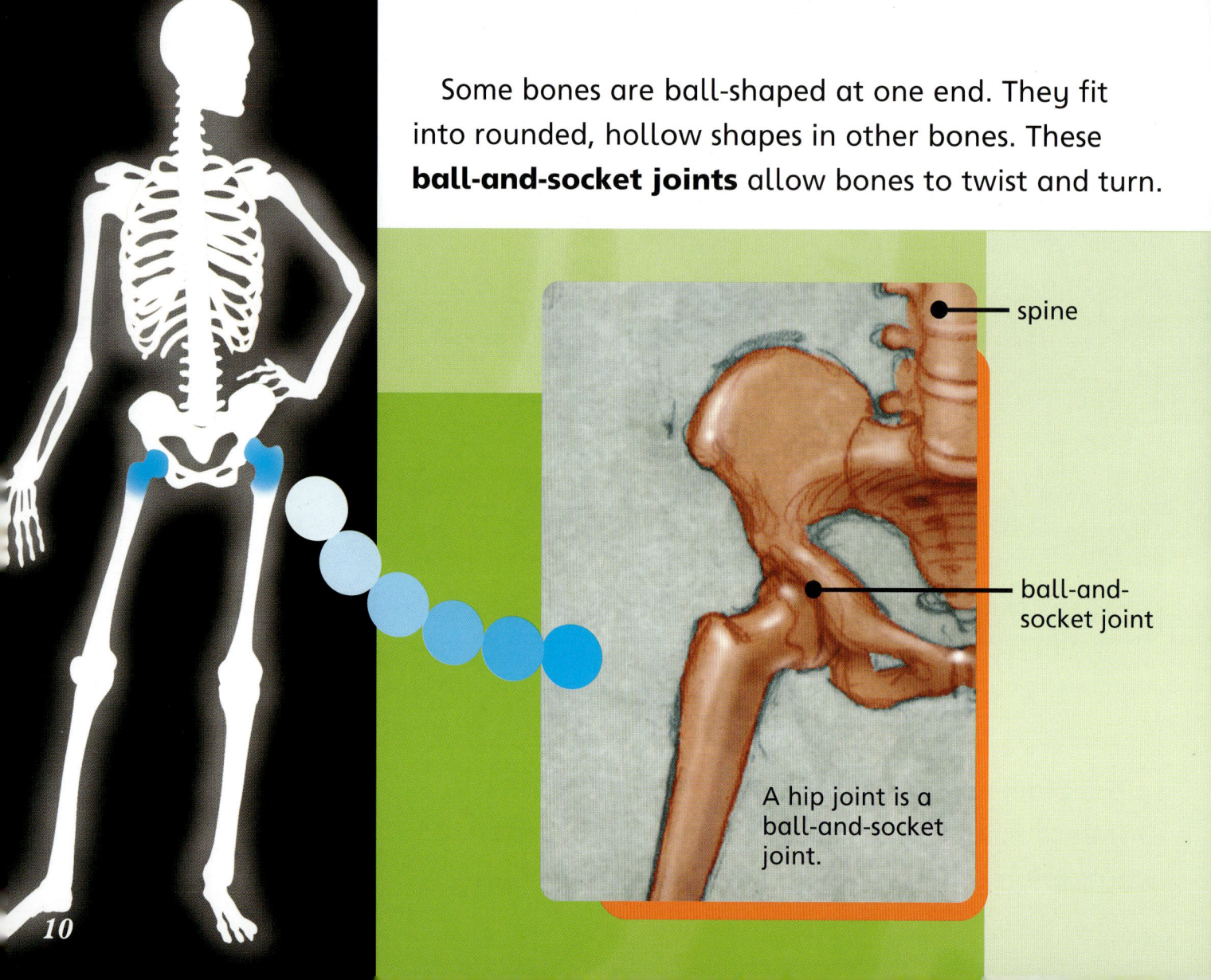

Some bones are ball-shaped at one end. They fit into rounded, hollow shapes in other bones. These **ball-and-socket joints** allow bones to twist and turn.

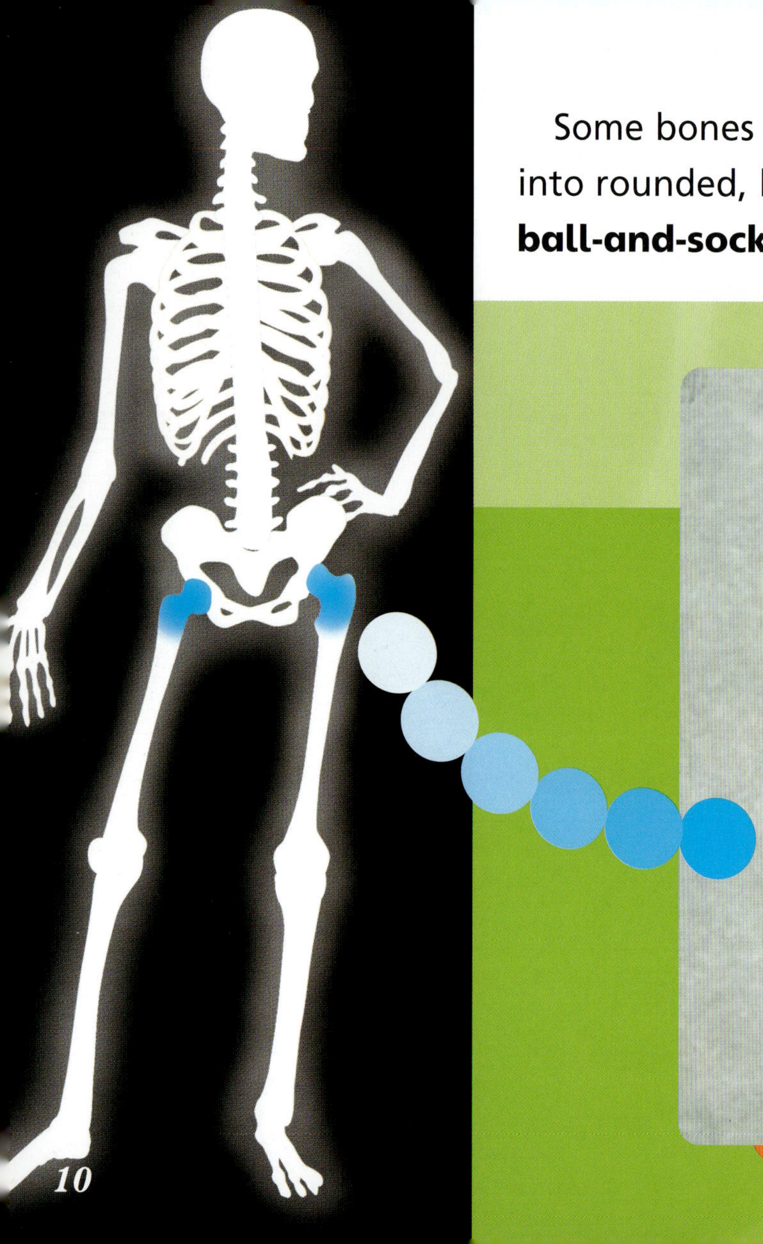

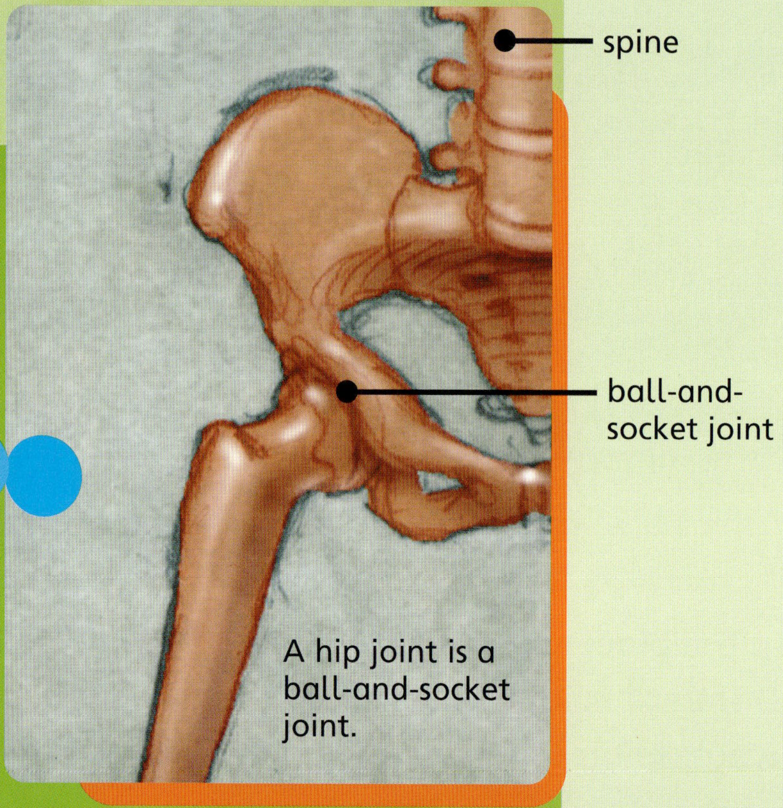

A hip joint is a ball-and-socket joint.

ball-and-socket joint

spine

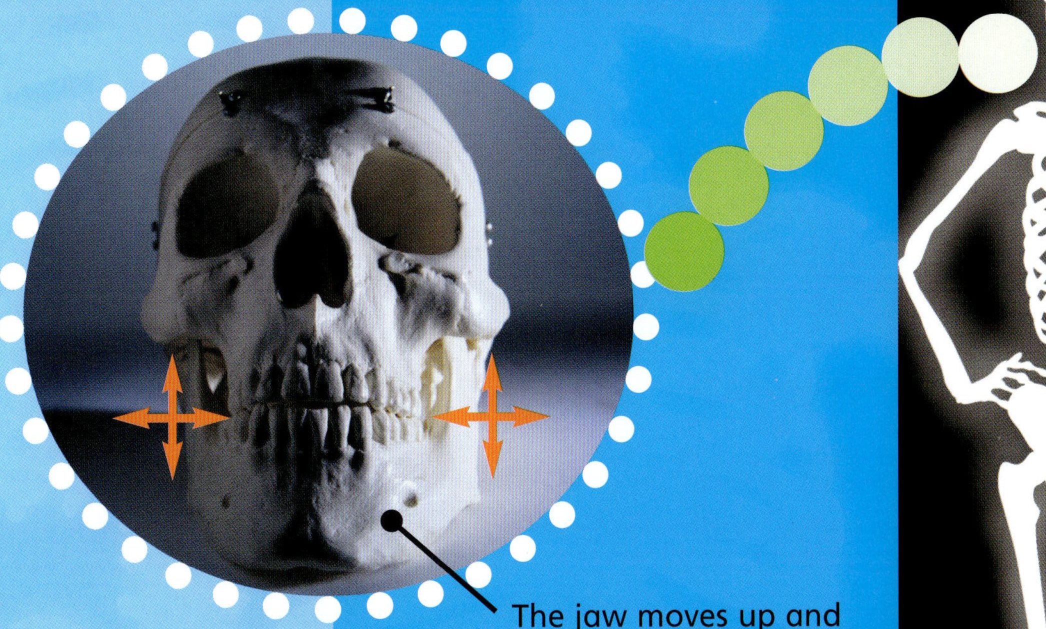

11

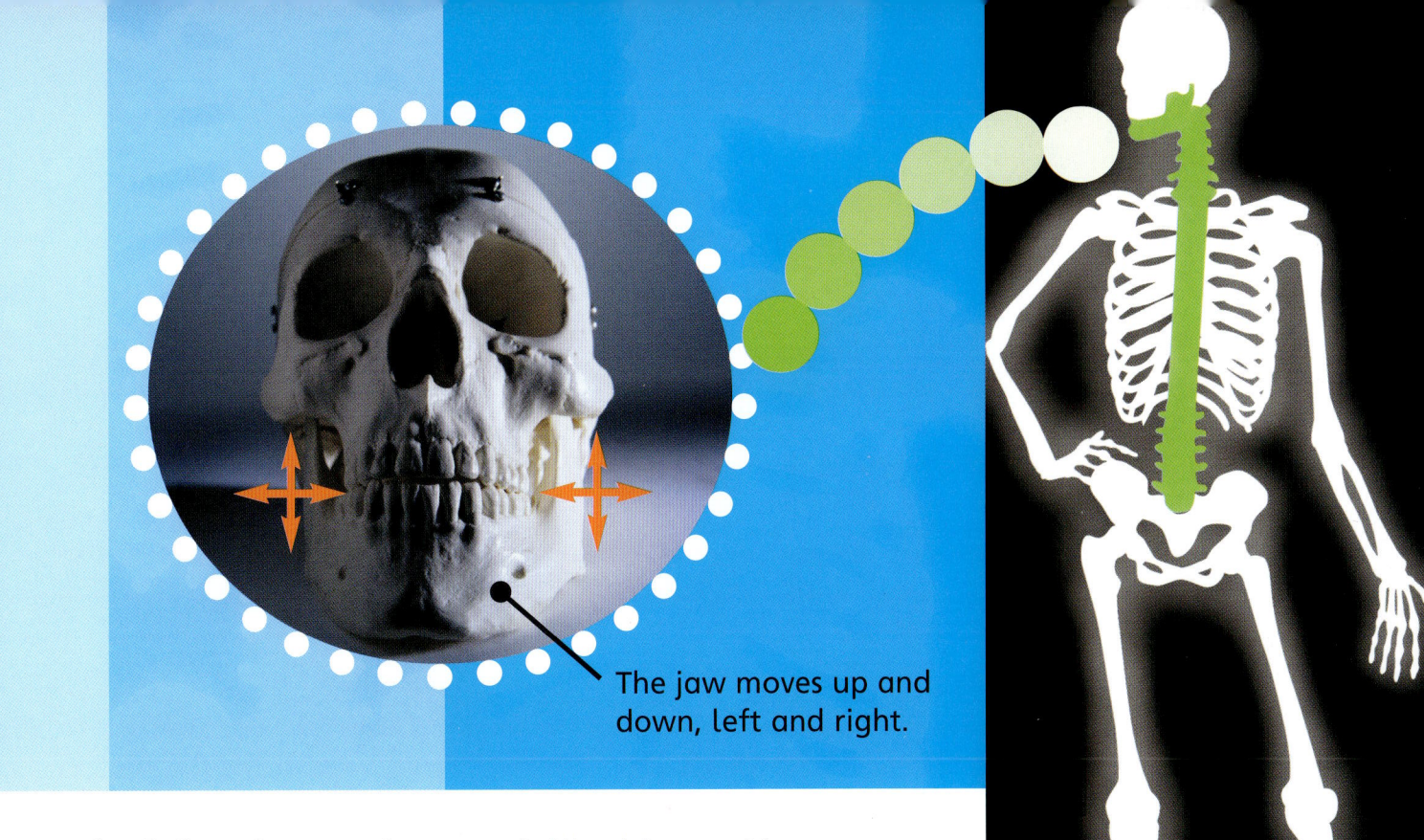

The jaw moves up and down, left and right.

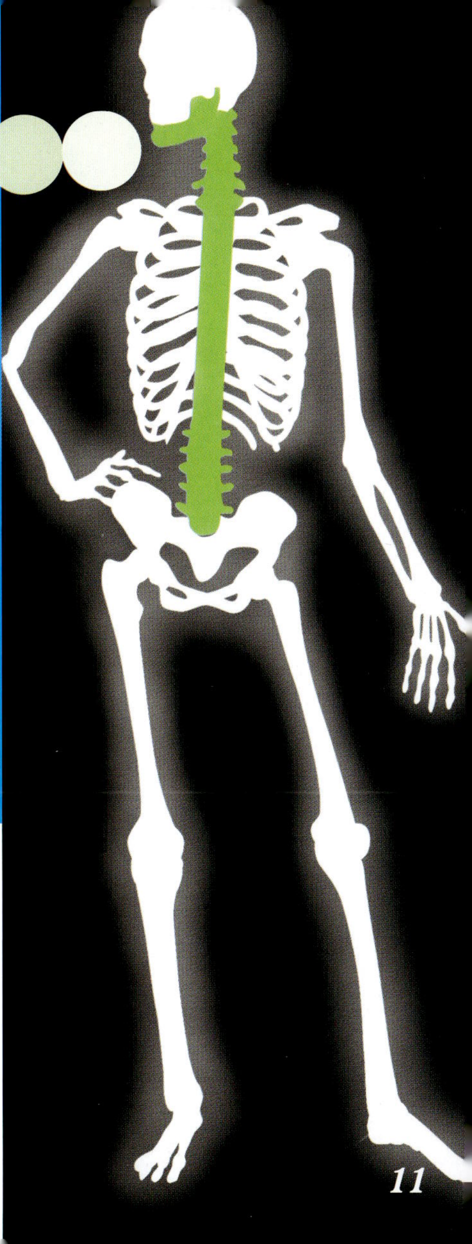

The **joints** in your jaw work like hinges. Your lower jaw bone can move up and down, and from side to side, to help you bite and chew.

The joints in your **spine** help the bones slide over one another so that you can bend.

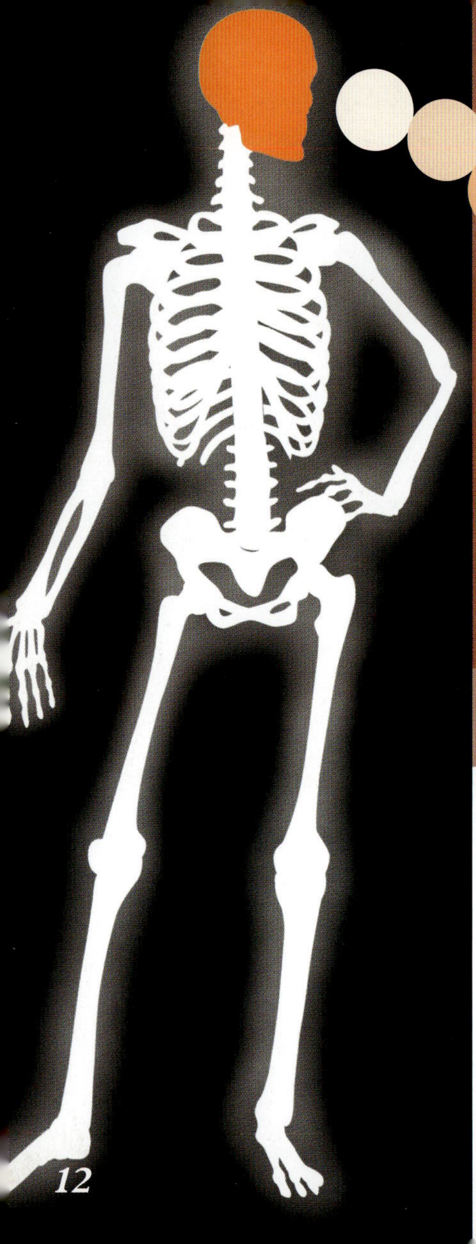

Flat, curved bones fit together to make the top part of your **skull**. They protect your brain from bumps, which could cause damage.

The bones of your skull also give your face its shape. They hold your teeth in place. The muscles of your face are attached to the skull bones.

Skull

Skull, front view

Skull, top view

Spine

An S-shaped chain of small bones fit together to make your **spine**. Your spine is strong enough to hold up your heavy head. Your spine protects important **nerves**. It holds your body upright over your legs and feet.

Side of spine

Back of spine

Front of spine

Pelvis

Your **pelvis** is made of large, flat, curved bones. These bones protect important **organs** in your body like the **bladder**. Your pelvis joins your legs to your body and helps your body balance, too.

An X-ray of a pelvis

Ribs

Rib bones are narrow. They make the 'cage' of your chest and back. They protect your heart and lungs. They move up and down as you breathe.

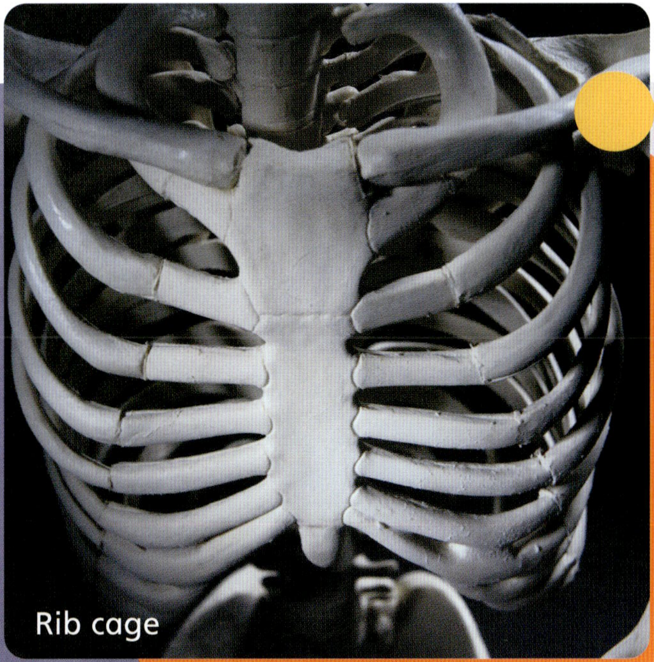

Rib cage

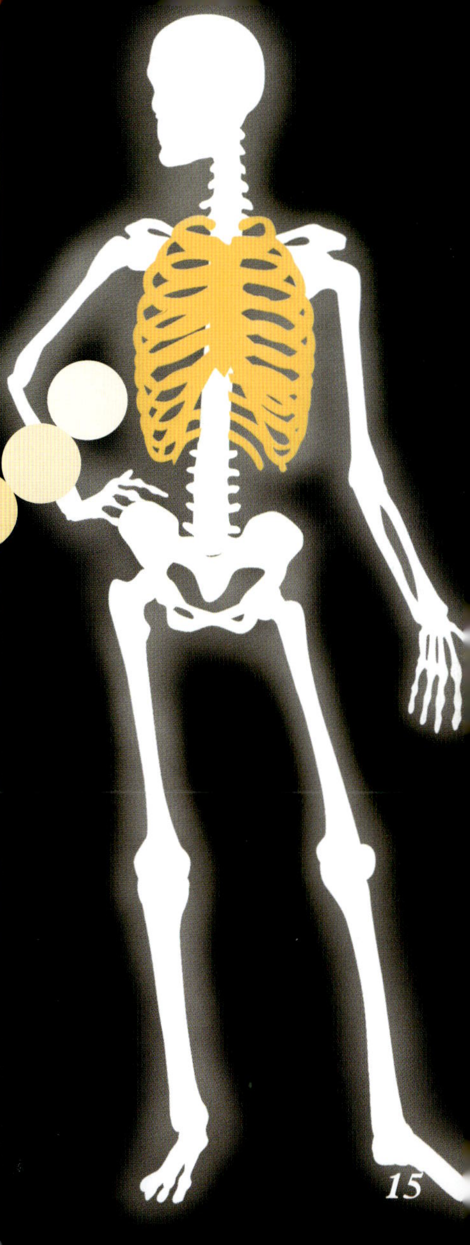

15

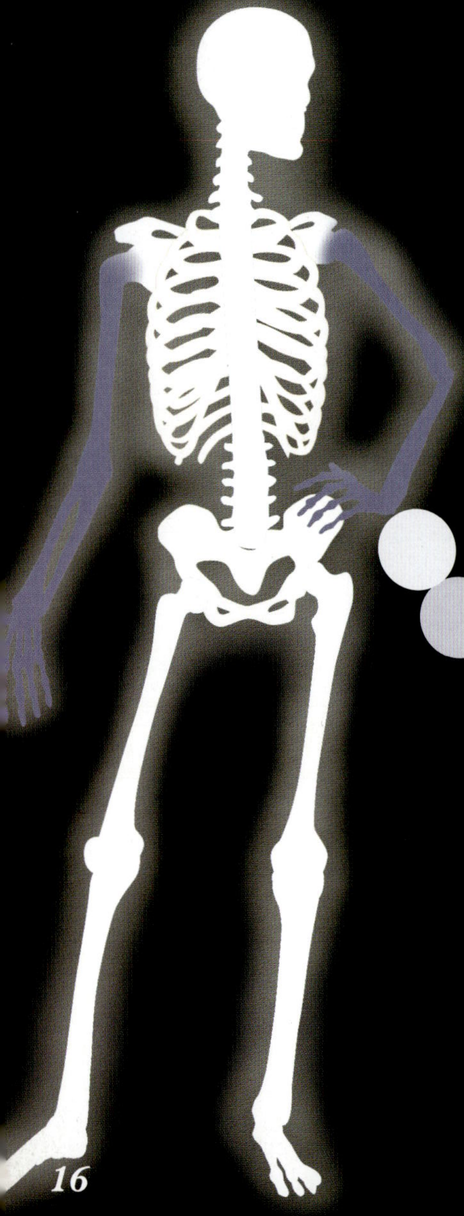

Arms and Hands

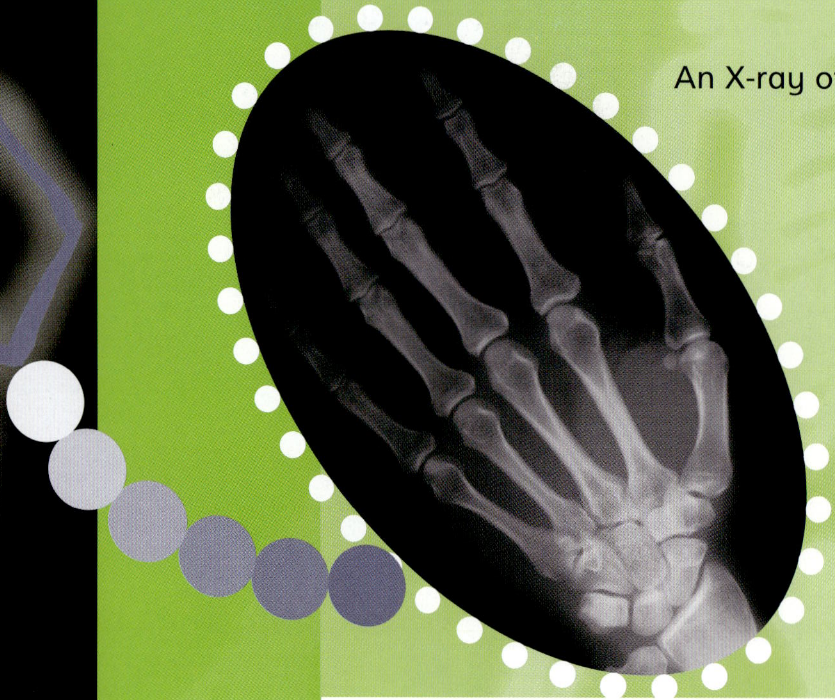

Arm bones are long and strong. They help you lift and carry things. Hands are made up of small bones that can move in many different ways, allowing you to grip and move objects.

An X-ray of a hand

Legs and Feet

Leg bones are very strong. They hold up the weight of your body. Your thigh bones are the longest bones in your body.

The small bones in your feet help you balance. They also help carry the weight of your body.

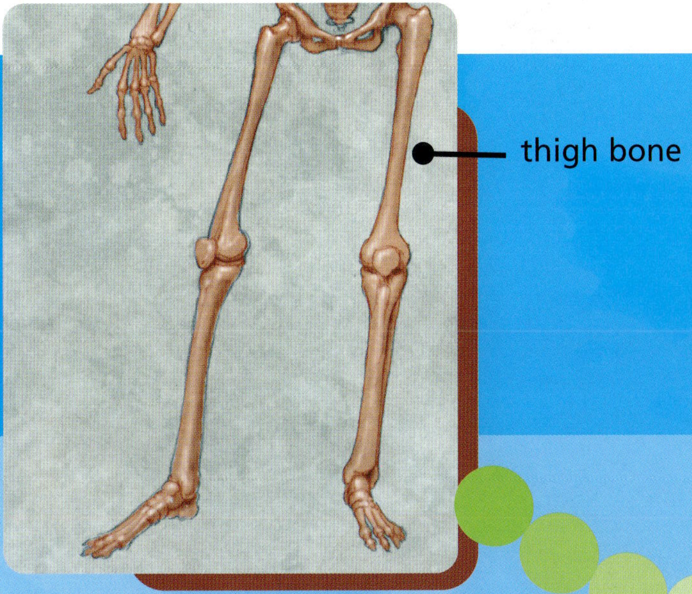

thigh bone

Over half of the 206 bones in the body are found in the hands and feet.

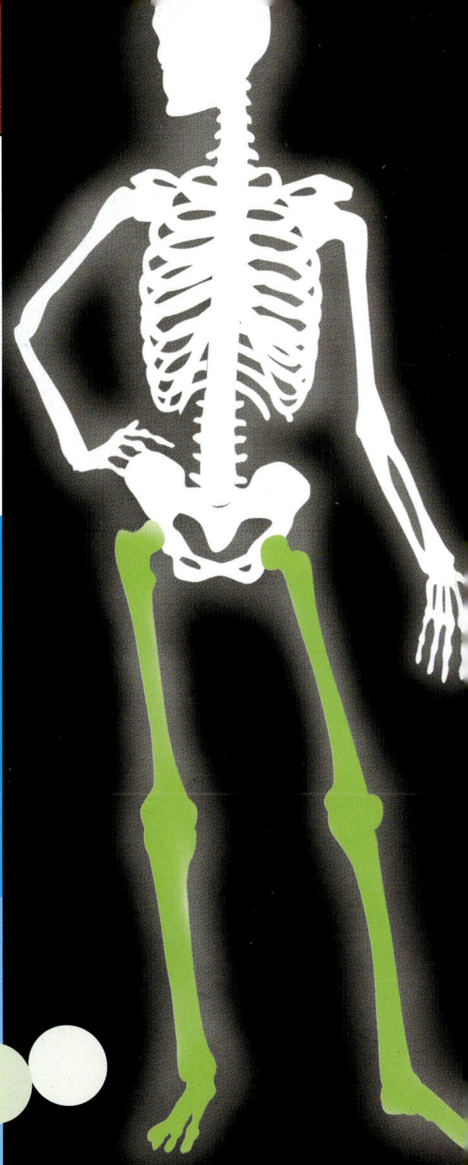

17

Broken Bones

Bones are strong, but they can break if too much pressure is put on them. If you fall, or if something falls on you, you may end up with a broken bone. This is called a **fracture**.

Interesting Bone Fact

A bone is five times stronger than a steel bar of the same weight.

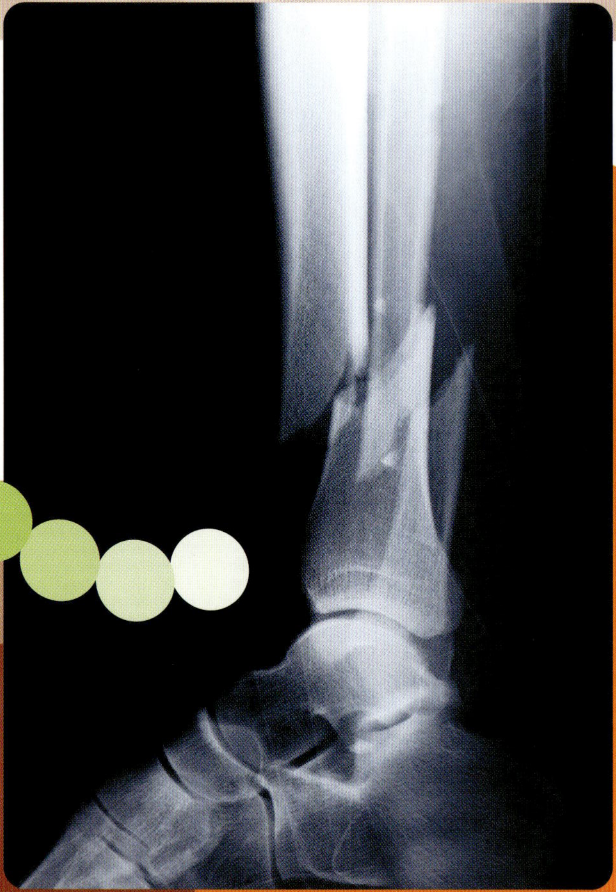

A fractured leg bone

Types of Fracture

Hairline fracture — A very fine, thin break

Complete fracture — When the bone breaks into two separate pieces

Greenstick fracture — When the bone splinters

Serious fractures happen when a bone breaks in more than one place or when it is crushed. Luckily, your skeleton is good at mending itself. New **cells** rebuild broken bones. They cover broken ends and close up breaks.

The X-ray machine will show if this girl has a fracture.

X-ray machine

Some broken bones are given a helping hand to mend. To help them mend in just the right way, a doctor sets the broken bone into its normal position. An X-ray helps the doctor see the break in the bone. The X-ray is a special photograph of the inside of your body. After the doctor sets the bone, it is kept in place with a **cast** or metal pins.

A doctor examining X-rays

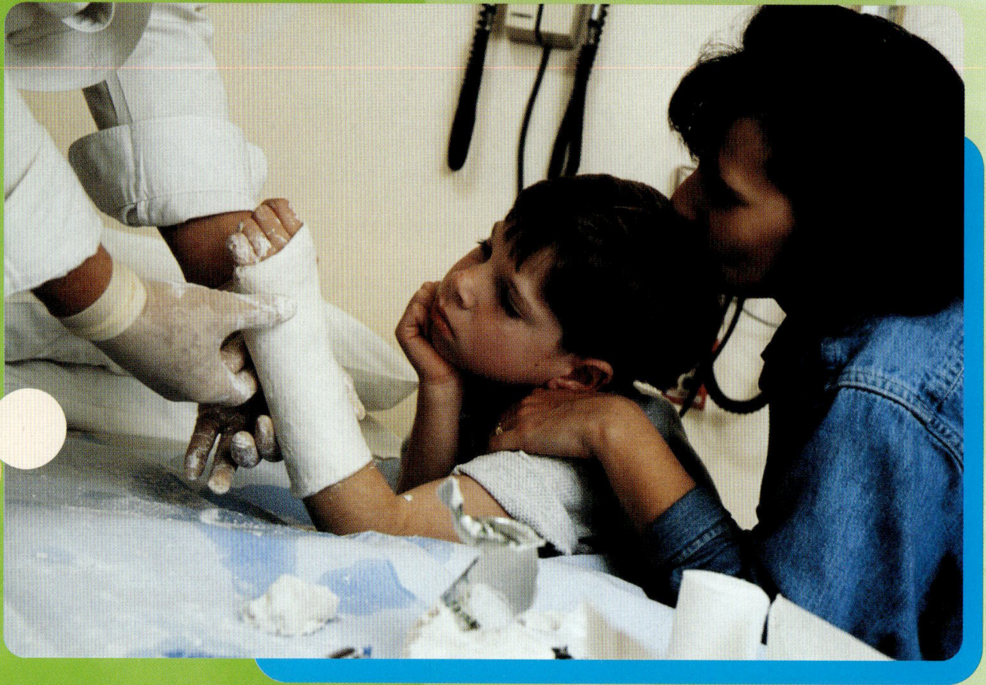

A **cast** can be made of plaster and bandages, plastic or fibreglass. Some casts are waterproof, which means you can still swim, shower and bath while you are wearing them. When the broken bone has mended, the cast is taken off.

This cast will keep the boy's wrist bones in place while they heal.

Glossary

ball-and-socket joint – A joint in which the rounded end of one bone fits into the rounded hollow of another bone.

bladder – A bag that stores urine in the body.

brittle – Easily broken.

cartilage – Soft material that may harden into bone.

cast – A case for holding a broken bone in place as it mends.

cells – The tiniest part of a living thing.

fracture – A break in a bone.

joint – The place where bones meet.

nerves – Parts of the body that carry messages from your brain to other parts of your body.

organs – The inside parts of your body, each with their own special job that helps the body function.

pelvis – Large bowl-shaped bones at the base of your spine.

ribs – A cage of bones in your chest and back.

skull – The bones that cover your brain and give your head its shape.

spine – The line of bones that runs from the base of your brain to the lower part of your back. Your spine is also called your backbone.

Index

animal/s 3, 7
babies 5, 8
balance 14, 17
bone/s 3-22
cartilage 8
cast 21, 22
cells 6, 20
fracture/s 18-20
humans 3, 5
joint/s 4, 9-11
skeleton/s 3, 5, 7, 20
skull 4, 12
spine 4, 10, 11, 13
X-ray/s 9, 14, 16, 20, 21